WOTTON UNDER-EDGE
TO
CHIPPING SODBURY
IN OLD PHOTOGRAPHS

DETAIL OF CHILDREN at Rounceval Street, Chipping Sodbury, see page 145.

WOTTON UNDER-EDGE
TO
CHIPPING SODBURY
IN OLD PHOTOGRAPHS

COLLECTED BY
ALAN SUTTON

ALAN SUTTON
1987

Alan Sutton Publishing Limited
Brunswick Road · Gloucester

First published 1987

British Library Cataloguing in Publication Data

Wotton-under-Edge to Chipping Sodbury in
old photographs.
1. Chipping Sodbury Region (Gloucestershire)
—History   2. Wotton-under-Edge Region
(Gloucestershire)—History
I. Sutton, Alan
942.3′91   DA690.C545/

ISBN 0-86299-389-X

Typesetting and origination by
Alan Sutton Publishing Limited.
Printed in Great Britain
by WBC Print Limited · Bristol

CONTENTS

POSED PHOTOGRAPH of an organ grinder, probably by the Wotton photographer A. Durn
c.1901.

INTRODUCTION

In 1901 there were one million five hundred thousand domestic servants in Great Britain. As most of the photographs in this book are from around this period think what activity there was behind the bricks and mortar. There were scullery maids, cooks, housemaids; and in the larger houses, gardeners, housekeepers and other staff to do the bidding of the old social order – an order greatly disrupted and never quite the same after the First World War.

This was just one of my thoughts as I spent many happy hours looking at photographs through a magnifying glass, trying to read shop signs and other fascinating detail. Take, for instance, the picture of the boy with the hoop. The crook and hoop together with his hat and the cut of his coat would tempt me to date this to c.1880; and yet what a wealth of other information there is to glean from this one image. Local historians of now and the future will not have just the dry written word in the nineteenth-century trade directories of Hunt & Co., Pigot and Kelly; they will be able to see where the tradesmen operated from. They will see the bearded Mr. Hancock outside his chemist shop, the old lady pushing a bath chair as she did her marketing, the errand boy with his cap and wicker basket; the three, aproned artisans and the telegraph boy with cap and bag. With other shop proprietors, top hatted and straw hatted passers by, they all stop on this sunny day at seventeen minutes past ten to watch this strange 'image taking' character with a box on a stand covered by a black drape. They would all have realised that it was a photographer; but I doubt if any of them gave a thought that they were looking at their descendants, and that the lens was capturing not just a record of the day, but a record for posterity. Think of it. When you look at this picture, all eyes are focussed on you.

Old photographs have different meanings for all of us. For me, some pictures bring back evocative memories of sunny childhood days – picking blackcurrants in grandfather's garden, and the recollection of the heady fragrant smell of an avenue of lime trees in May and June as I made my way to school. As these memories are to me, so must everyone have their own evocation created from a simple image of times past and places changed. Many photographs show friends and relations almost as different people, before time has wreaked its inevitable toll. The street scenes in many pictures show our towns and villages in previous stages

of the constant metamorphic transition, with old buildings being demolished for new – which in turn become old and inevitably once more threatened, whilst the shopkeepers change their signs, and sometimes their premises, with son taking over from father, and son becoming a father and continuing the chain. In this book we can see elements of all of this. We see the father, with his young son in the doorway of the shop. We see the son – now grown and now the proud proprietor of a grocers' emporium. In turn we see him lose his hair and grow rotund – giving up his bicycle and acquiring a little Austin tourer to drive up the dusty dirt roads that still made up the streets, lanes and highways of our district.

Who were the photographers that captured these images so long ago? The camera was a rare and often hand-made affair in the nineteenth century, but in this area of Wotton and Sodbury we have the happy coincidence of Francis Frith and Murray Dowding lending their photographic skills, a double act that has made the compilation of this volume less difficult than it could well have been.

The story of Francis Frith is long and interesting, but space in this introduction allows only a brief summary. Frith was born in 1821 and started his career as a painter. His paintings were 'photographic' in the sense that his choice of viewpoint and the precision of his detail and perspective are consistent with the photographs that he made of similar scenes. He became interested in the new photographic process, then in its infancy; and set out to produce as complete a photographic record as he could of England from the mid-nineteenth-century onwards. Luckily for posterity, this archive is still available and well preserved.

In 1850 Frith founded F. Frith & Company, Photographic Printers and Publishers in his home town of Reigate in Surrey. From small beginnings the firm built up an extensive library of towns, villages and other views; and at the time of Frith's death in 1898 the company had an extensive command of the picture postcard market.

In a sense, our interest here is not with Francis, but his son Eustace. Although Francis took Gloucestershire pictures in his peripatetic tours, it was the farsightedness of Eustace that we need to thank.

Most of the company's postcards were printed in Germany using the collotype process. This is a process that produces images in a continuous tone instead of the 'screened' principle of producing an image made up of minute dots. Eustace started a collotype works at Charfield for the Frith company, but from the start this proved to be uneconomic and difficult to manage. In the end, the family decided to close the operation and finally severed their connection in 1907. Three senior employees decided to struggle on with the equipment and bought the operation from the Friths. Thus, in May 1909 the Cotswold Publishing Company was formed. The equipment was moved to new (old) premises – Britannia Mill at Wotton-under-Edge; and it is the photographic output from the Cotswold Publishing Company that has been so useful in this book. In 1919 the Frith connection was re-established when Francis Frith's grandson, Francis E. Frith joined the company. The Cotswold Publishing Company then won back the printing of Frith postcards

as well as publishing their own 'Cotswold' series. The picture here is of Britannia Mill in the 1920s, the man in the centre is preparing a collotype plate.

Our interest in Murray Dowding of Chipping Sodbury is of equal importance, but luckily for space here in this introduction, is much easier to relate. Dowding was born in 1881, the seventh child of a Chipping Sodbury plumber and ironmonger, Marcus Ridley Dowding. Murray started his working life with a Bristol engineering company, but after a bout of meningitis which nearly claimed his life, he joined his sister who was running the family firm following the early death of their father. His growing interest in photography around the turn of the century can be seen from two views of the family ironmongery business on page 129. The top view shows the shop before the First World War as an Ironmonger's selling paints, varnishes, lamps and cutlery etc. The bottom view shows that by 1920 the business includes the selling of stationery and local views as well as 'Films D & P'.

Murray Dowding, if not eccentric was certainly idiosyncratic. He had an obvious interest in local history, and a look through the Dowding glass negative archive at Bailey's in Dursley shows up this bias. He was also very keen on churches and church architecture – although the family had a strong nonconformist background. Perhaps the greatest impression to be formed on anyone viewing the archive is the fixation with William Tyndale, the translator of the bible. Dowding often gave an illustrated talk on Tyndale, and perhaps the propensity towards this subject was no more than many others, of which only the Tyndale material has survived.

Dowding did not have the flair of Francis Frith senior, or some of his own contemporary photographers. His pictures are rather stale, and – dare I say it – boring. However, having admitted my own feeling towards them I cannot say for

MURRAY DOWDING, and his dog Puck c.1916.

sure that I could have done any better; and Chipping Sodbury and Yate would surely be much the poorer without this early twentieth century archive. His posing of the Light North Lancs. sentry entitled 'In Time of War' is one of his better pictures, as is his 'View at Yate Rocks' showing the maid with her pail and the workman, homeward bound. The Love Lane Turnpike shows a rather posed family group, together with Dowding's own dog, Puck, to the right; in fact Puck accompanied Dowding on many trips, and remains to this day one of the world's most photographed dogs.

Apart from the Frith and Dowding postcards, there were other, more minor series from Bailey's, Page's and Price. Some shops even commissioned their own cards of local views. But postcards are not the only source of material; photographs were taken for all sorts of occasions, and in this book I have tried to achieve a reasonable balance between the postcard views and individual photographs.

Finally, I hope that this book will bring back happy memories to older folk who will recall scenes which have long been changed or gone, and that it will be of interest to the younger generations of now and to come, and to newcomers to this burgeoning housing area. I hope within a few years to be able to issue a follow-up volume, so if any reader has a picture they think may be of interest, please do let me know.

Alan Sutton
Hydefield
Uley

From North Nibley to the Ridge and on to Old Town

JAMES TALBOYS' HORSE AND CART, c.1910. I have not been able to find out much about this picture, presumably it is North Nibley. Is the young man James Talboys, his son, or an employee? The date is a calculated guess from the costume.

North Nibley, showing R. Severn.

NORTH NIBLEY from Nibley Knoll, a view taken in 1906. This view is from a postcard in the Frith's series, and must have been one of the last to have been printed by their own collotype press at Charfield. The Severn can be seen in the distance.

North Nibley, and Tyndale's Memorial.

NORTH NIBLEY in 1904. This view, towards Tyndale's monument and the Knoll is also looking at the point from which the above picture was taken. The shop window on the right is advertising Zebra Grate Polish and Huntley & Palmers biscuits.

THE BLACK HORSE INN, 1915. The lettering on the side reads:
THE
BLACK HORSE
INN
W. HARPER
RETAILER BEER WINES SPIRITS
GOOD STABLING
HORSES   ACCOMMODATION
CARRIAGES   FOR CYCLISTS

The sign in the middle is for Dunlop tyres.

The trader's carriage is advertising tea sets, and is obviously well loaded with galvanized baths, buckets etc.

THE RIDGE, the south-east façade and main entrance, c.1930.

THE RIDGE BILLIARD ROOM, 1904.

THE RIDGE, the south-west side and orangery c.1910. This imposing house was designed by George Stanley Repton, the son of landscape gardener Humphry Repton, and the pupil of architect John Nash. The Ridge was one of Repton's first commissions, and was received from Edward Sheppard, a Uley Clothier. The house was designed in 1825 and presumably completed shortly afterwards, but by 1837 Sheppard was bankrupt; the victim of the cloth trade depression. It was then bought by George Bengough, a Bristol banker; and stayed in the Bengough family until 1900. After a short spell as a country club, it was finally demolished in 1936 and sold off as building materials.

DEMOLISHING THE RIDGE, 1936. Note the lions from the main façade as shown on page 17.

COOMBE, c. 1910.

COOMBE ROAD in the 1950s.

COOMBE ROAD before 1900, note the scholar with his mortar board! The sign on the wall is for The Coach and Horses Inn. The building behind was Andrews and Lacey's Forge. See page 22.

WOTTON GAS WORKS C.1945 with the Cedars behind.

THE CEDARS, probably in the first decade of the century. Unlike the picture above, the house at this time retained its elegance – and, of course, its cedar trees.

WOTTON CARRIAGE BUILDERS c.1900. Before the age of motor cars, each town had wheelwrights, some of whom also built wagons and carriages. In the Hunt & Co. Directory of 1849, no less than six wheelwrights are listed for Wotton-under-Edge.

ST. MARY THE VIRGIN, the parish church for Wotton; a view taken from the top floor of the Britannia Mill c.1900. The church has an original consecration date of 1283, but much of the fabric carries a later date.

Wotton-under-Edge Church. West front.

ST. MARY THE VIRGIN. A view of the west front c.1905.
The lower two stages of the tower are fourteenth century, the upper two are Perpendicular.
David Verey in his Gloucestershire volumes of *The Buildings of England* calls St. Mary's tower

     '. . . one of the most splendid Perpendicular towers in the county.'

ST. MARY THE VIRGIN. The church porch c.1905. This porch was rebuilt in 1658, the window is to the priest's chamber over the porch, added during the rebuilding.

THE COURT HOUSE, a photograph of 1950 showing this ancient house with its added-on eighteenth-century façade. The house has since been carefully restored.

A PROCESSION IN OLD TOWN, C. 1911. The band is probably the Abbey Band of Kingswood, who wore a distinctive 'AB' badge at the front of their caps.

WOTTON'S FIRST BUS. This vehicle ran between Wotton and Charfield, and superseded the horse drawn bus. The bus is stationary here at Old Town, the driver enjoying a cigarette. The sign at the back of the bus against the wall is advertising Schweppes Dry Ginger Ale, whilst the sun vizor in front of the driver advertizes Ideal Milk, both names still very familiar to us.

OLD TOWN MEETING HOUSE, c.1895. Originally built between 1701 and 1703, the Meeting House was greatly improved in 1800, in the early eighteenth century, the Meeting House was greatly improved in 1800, side galleries were built and a chancel added on; giving a seating capacity of some 300. Note the windows in this picture. These were removed during further work in 1903, and replaced with tall lancet windows.

A VIEW OF WOTTON FROM BLACKQUARRIES HILL, 1905.

LOOKING DOWN OLD TOWN, towards the War Memorial, c.1920.

OLD TOWN c.1900, a gas lamp standing where the War Memorial was subsequently built.

Around
Wotton Streets

THE CLOUD. This was the original area of 'Wudetun', the Saxon 'Wood Town', destroyed by fire during the reign of King John in the early thirteenth century.

POTTER'S POND. This picture, together with that of the Cloud opposite was taken in the first decade of this century. The cottages on the right are also shown to the right, opposite. They look quite picturesque, but life would have been far different from what we are used to today. Most accommodation would have been rented, and so repairs were always slow to be done – see the roof of the cottage to the left. No cottage would have had a damp course, and the solid floors would have been flag stones lain straight onto the earth. Cold in winter, damp and sweaty in the summer.

The water supply would have been from wells – piped supply did not begin until 1894. Toilets would have been earth closets, or over cess pits – which often leaked into wells! The major cholera outbreak of 1849 which killed 25 people particularly affected this quarter of town.

THE OLD GRAMMAR SCHOOL. This photograph of Katherine Lady Berkeley's Grammar School was taken some time shortly prior to 1900 before the façade was altered. The scalloped door canopy was removed to the Bluecoat School, Culverhay. Here it was subsequently 'removed' by a lorry! The present version is a fibre glass replica.

The exposure on this picture was obviously lengthy to judge by the figures – both wearing traditional costume.

Parish Church and Potters Pond, Wotton-U-Edge

POTTER'S POND. A postcard view c.1915.

POTTER'S POND. The Morley family, c.1890.

SYNWELL. A view c.1920.

CHURCH STREET, c.1920, looking towards Long Street and showing the shops of Charles Ellery and W.H. Thomas.

CHURCH STREET. Two views looking towards Old Town. These pictures are interesting as they show how the camera can so effectively lie. Both pictures were taken from a similar spot, but with different lenses. The top picture c.1880, the bottom picture c.1900. Nothing much has changed. The Jolly Reaper is on the right hand side in both views; a gas lamp is new on the left hand side of the bottom view. Note in the bottom picture the old lady in traditional costume entering the almshouse.

THE FALCON HOTEL, c.1870. Joseph Derrett was landlord of the White Lion in 1849, and James Derrett ran the Pack Horse Inn at the end of the century; which one is this? Or was there a third J. Derrett?

CHURCH STREET. Charles Ellery's grocery store in 1906. Charles Ellery is on the right, his delivery boy, Dick Pagett to his right hand.

LUDGATE HILL c.1900.

IMPERIA CLOTHING. W.H. Thomas' clothing and drapery empire on the corner of Church Street and Long Street, c.1905.

LONG STREET c.1900, the shop signs on the right read 'Fowles Outfitter' and further up 'Cridland'.

LONG STREET. Both of these pictures were taken within a year or so of each other c.1924. See if you can discover the give-away clue to show which is the older.

INDIA & CHINA TEA COMPANY, Long Street. The signs for this shop can be seen in the previous pictures slightly further up on the left hand side of the road. Although the original of this was somewhat damaged, it has considerable charm and I could not resist including it. The Company later changed premises, moving further down Long Street, a few doors up from the post office.

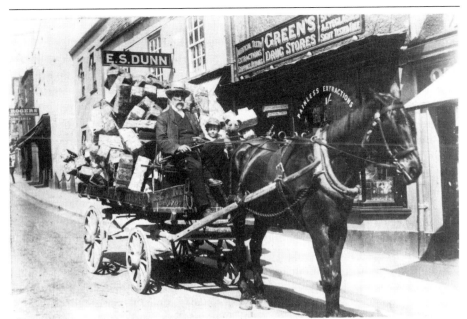

LONG STREET, Mr R. Morley and Harry Morley, some time shortly before 1922. The house further up the street next to Messrs. E.S. Dunn was the old Grantley House.

GRANTLEY HOUSE, a few years before the shop front was inserted.

THE FAIR COMES TO TOWN! A fairground vehicle making its way up Long Street and into The Chipping c.1910.

LONG STREET, the junction with Market Street c.1925.

EVERYTHING STOPS FOR THE CAMERA. Long Street c.1880, Parker's decorating supplies shop on the left with the rocking horse above the shop front. The camera at this date must have been something of a novelty, and the exposures would have been lengthy. To get everyone clear in this picture they must have been posed; only the little girl on the left hand side not managing to be patient! M.A. Parker was presumably the son of George William Parker who is listed in the 1849 directory as a painter, plumber and glazier in Wickwar.

CARNIVAL IN TOWN. A Long Street procession c.1905.

KING GEORGE V JUBILEE CELEBRATION, 1935 The White Lion, suitably decorated for the occasion. As well as offering the usual refreshments, the White Lion was also a filling station, taxi hire depot, parcels receiving depot and coach station! The White Lion once had its own brewery, which still stands at the back, with an entrance from Bear Street.

Standing in the doorway is the landlady Mrs Scadding with her eldest daughter, Phyllis. On the right of the doorway is the landlord Mr T.A.V. Scadding with his son, Douglas. The little girl is Hazel Scadding with dog, Judy.

LONG STREET, LOOKING INTO HIGH STREET, c.1880. See the introduction for details.

The White Lion has its old façade here. The present building, although looking relatively modern has a medieval framework, the new frontage being built at the turn of the century, and the interior was also modernised to some extent.

HIGH STREET. A postcard view c.1905. Note the perspective between this picture and that on page 46. The camera angle can be deceptive.

HIGH STREET and the corner of Haw Street c.1904, F.W. Fry, the insurance broker, outside his office. See page 74.

MARKET STREET, showing Victoria House and the Tolsey, some time after 1887, the year in which the new clock was provided in celebration of Queen Victoria's Golden Jubilee. The golden dragon on top of the Tolsey cupola dates from 1859, the previous cupola and dragon being declared unsafe.

THE TOWN HALL, before the restoration work of 1870. The work undertaken in 1870 left the building less attractive than before; the dormer windows were removed and the ground floor altered.

The picture below shows the Town Hall after the restoration work of 1870, but before further work undertaken in 1884, when the ground floor was totally enclosed and split up into rooms.

MARKET STREET. This is probably the oldest photograph in this book, as it must have been taken some time before 1863, when the buildings opposite the Swan were demolished. Presumably this was done to widen the street; it would be interesting to know why this one building alone jutted out, breaking up the street line.

Photography before 1863 was rare. The picture shown here is quite clear considering the lengthy exposure time that would have been necessary.

Careful observation of pictures such as this can throw light on alterations to the street scene. We know the picture is of 1863 or before, and because of this, even without other documentary evidence we can tell that the ground floor shop front to Hancock's druggist store was put in after this date. Looking carefully down Market Street it can be seen to be a doorway with a window on each side; compare this with the shop front in enlarged picture on pages 8 and 9.

MARKET STREET BEFORE 1870. This picture shows the street decorated for one of the town flower shows. The bus on the right-hand-side plied between the Swan and Charfield station. The picture is after 1863, but before 1870. Can you find the clue? The answer is on page 159.

THE CHIPPING. Although this is not a photograph, it shows the rather charming scene of the Chipping as it would have looked in the latter half of the nineteenth century and before. Well House, later known as Chipping House is, obviously enough, the house behind the well. After the cholera epidemic of 1854 the well was closed, and only re-opened after a spell of eleven years.

MR RICHINGS, the butcher, with horse and cart in the Chipping. His shop was in Long Street, see page 39.

A VIEW ACROSS THE CHIPPING, c.1890. Taken from the entrance to the Chipping School, looking across to Well House and Market Street. The Chipping was grassed at this time. The single storey building in the background was Penley's Firework Manufactory.

FUN-FAIR AT THE CHIPPING. This picture is not easy to date; from the lady with the hoops, and the boys' costume, I would plump for c.1900.

THE FUN-FAIR IN TOWN. This picture is a little later, probably c.1910. The fair was usually at the Chipping, but the large tree in the background makes this rather doubtful in this instance. The boys seem more interested in the camera than the act.

HAW STREET, C.1905. This view, looking south-west towards Charfield and Kingswood must have been taken some years after 1896 as the sign for the Pack Horse Inn has gone and the road has been remade with new guttering slabs. Note the thin-sash windows, a feature of some Wotton buildings.

HAW STREET, C.1890. This view is looking in the same direction as the previous picture, but is taken from the north side of the street. The Pack Horse was first recorded in existence in 1755. In 1871 it was a posting house, and was last documented in 1896.

A SIGN OF THE FIRST WORLD WAR IN HAW STREET. A convoy of Thornycroft army lorries, possibly even the same convoy shown in Chipping Sodbury; see page 141.

HAW STREET, c.1890. This view taken looking north-east towards Rowland Hill's tabernacle.

HAW STREET, detail of page 57 showing the police station and the tabernacle.

MUDDY ROADS AND FOOTSCRAPERS. This fine photograph of Haw Street illustrates the conditions of the roads at the end of the nineteenth century. Many houses of previous centuries that are still standing often have footscrapers built into the wall, or to one or other side of the door. Nowadays they are redundant, but this pictures shows a time when they were clearly necessary.

MR 'TOZZY' WATTS AND FAMILY, outside their Bradley Road shop c.1900.

FIRST WORLD WAR POSTERS, in Gloucester Street, probably near the beginning of the war, as it is evident from the style of the posters that conscription was not yet compulsory.

MISS PRICE IN BEAR STREET. Note the shadow in the bottom right-hand-side of the picture. Is that the shadow of a delivery boy on a bicycle, lounging over his machine as he watches the photographer?

SECTION THREE
Wotton Pot-pourri

WOTTON CRICKET CLUB, two pictures from the end of the nineteenth century, probably taken about five to ten years apart. If the player in the top picture, first row, third from our left is the same player in the bottom picture, back row sixth from left; then my estimate is that the top picture is the older of the two!

SYNWELL A.F.C., cup winners 1909–1912.

A WOTTON FOOTBALL TEAM, c.1898.

WOTTON A.F.C., 1911–12 season.

THE WOTTON FIRE BRIGADE. This picture was taken in 1928 immediately after the Walk Mills fire. It was the inadequacy of managing at this fire which prompted the purchase of a new machine. The one shown in the picture here was bought in 1887 for £120. Standing on the left is Frank Ford, Landlord of the Star. Others are Edgar Jelliman, Orley Ford and Mr Jenkins. On a Saturday morning in September 1929 when the fire engine was to be named at a public ceremony it was called to a fire at the Cotswold Publishing Company at Britannia Mill. Owing to this fact the original name was scrapped and the engine named *Firefly*, having 'flown to a fire' when all was prepared for its naming ceremony.

THE PROUD BRIGADE, posed in front of their brand new machine.

THE BRAND NEW MACHINE. Rather an improvement on the 1887 model. This 1929 Dennis fire engine has recently (July 1987) been brought back to Wotton, but not to fight fires.

THE CHILDREN OF BEAR STREET SCHOOL. This 'class of 1954' has Mr Douglas Scadding standing on our left and Mr Carter, the headmaster, standing on our right. Douglas Scadding also appears in the picture on p.45.

THE CHIPPING SCHOOL. These two pictures are both very early, the top one probably c.1870. The school was built at the instigation of the church in 1837, as a National School for girls and infants.

KATHERINE LADY BERKELEY'S GRAMMAR SCHOOL. These two interior pictures were taken in 1950 during a campaign to obtain new premises; the attempt being made to highlight the cramped and antiquated conditions. Mr Rastell is the teacher in the top picture, and for all of you chemists, the writing on the board reads:– sodium hydroxide + sulphuric acid = sodium —?

CHURCH MILL. This mill, otherwise known as Steep Mill stood in Ludgate Hill. It was built in 1800–1802, and in its later years was used as overspill accommodation for Katherine Lady Berkeley's Grammar School. It was demolished in 1963 and the county library now stands on the site.

HACK MILL. This 1935 photograph shows the mill and the lido. Note the water polo goal.

HACK MILL POND, looking towards Wotton c.1905.

WOTTON LIDO! The lido on Hack Mill pond, almost the same view point as the picture above, and taken on the same day as the view on page 69.

WATER BABIES NEAR BRITANNIA MILL, in the summer of 1935. Amongst the group are Eric Hinder, Les Cornock, Massa Porter, Stan Oxenham, Bob Hedges, Stan Morris and Les James.

MR JOHN JOTCHAM'S WOTTON WORKMEN, C.1904. His building premises was behind what is now Lapham and Mann's in Market Street.

THE HANDS ON SHOVELS BRIGADE. Local roadmen c.1919. Obviously happy in their work.

AN EARLY STOKES BREAD VAN. This picture c.1924.

WOTTON TOWN HALL IN THE MID-1930s. Re-enactment of 'Dunmow Flitch' trial. Any married couple proving that they had lived in harmony for a year and a day were awarded the flitch of bacon.

A CHARABANC OUTING. This picture of the early 1920s shows a local outing in a charabanc, possibly one of the many Thornycroft army lorries that were remodelled after the end of the First World War.

MR F.W. FRY, the insurance broker and auctioneer inside his office in 1904. See page 47.

ELLERNCROFT. A family group, including Polly, c.1890.

A LOCAL CHARACTER. Probably a pose by a Wotton photographer.

THE SHEPHERD IN HIS SMOCK. Another local pose, probably by Mr A. Durn.

THE CEREMONY OF THE TEAPOTS! Probably a long service award ceremony for employees of Tubbs Lewis of over fifty years. This photograph was taken at 'Ellern Croft', the home of Sir Stanley and Lady Tubbs (shown centre).

CELEBRATIONS IN LONG STREET. There was some difference of opinion over this photograph. One was marked VJ Day, another was marked 'Coronation 1953'. To my mind, the fashion is too '1940s' for the coronation, and so it is either VE Day or VJ Day. I think it has to be VE Day, and I presume that the little girl in the front has her Churchillian salute around the wrong way; caught up in the enthusiasm for the moment!

Wortley and Alderley Hillesley and Hawkesbury

A VIEW OF WORTLEY IN 1905.

BROADBRIDGE MILL, c.1925; Mr A.C. Beale in the foreground.

ALDERLEY HOUSE, a postcard view of c.1910.

ALDERLEY STOCKS, another postcard view, this time slightly earlier at around 1900.

MONKS MILL, ALDERLEY. This Edwardian pose in the ruins of Monks Mill was for an early series of Cotswold Publishing Company postcards, probably c.1909. The girl's garb appears to be a cycling costume, designed to hide the ankles – even when pedalling.

MONKS MILL, ALDERLEY. This is an early postcard c.1900, although the photograph from which the view was taken may pre-date this by twenty years. Note the traditional costume of the woman on the right. Shortly after this view was taken, the mill suffered some structural collapse.

AN ALDERLEY POSTCARD VIEW, c.1905.

MR W.J. AND C.J. COATES, bakers and grocers of Hillesley, c.1921. This picture, and the one opposite at the top illustrate the difficulty to be experienced by any compiler of old photograph books. Just how do you date such pictures, which is the earlier? You look long and hard at each view, trying to find the giveaway clues that will reveal the answer. You look at the costume for clues. You even look at the moss on the slates or tiles to see which clump has grown larger thus showing some degree of time relevance. Luckily, in this case the original photograph has the pencil legend circa 1921 written on the back. Is this the truth, or somebody else's calculated guess? The picture opposite has the legend Mr J. Lyons written on the back of the original. I suspect that this is about twenty years older than the view above. The virginia creeper on the house behind is still growing in the opposite picture, yet in the view above it is rampant. Also, the above picture shows a light patch on the wall where ivy has been cleared away.

MR J. LYONS. See description opposite.

A VIEW OF HILLESLEY, c.1890, with Wotton-under-Edge in the background.

HILLESLEY, c.1910. A Cotswold Publishing Company postcard view.

THE FLEECE INN, Hillesley c.1915. With a soldier and his family? Looking towards the camera.

HAWKESBURY UPTON. The Plain and High Street, c.1910.

A MURRAY DOWDING VIEW OF HAWKESBURY, c.1920.

THE BADMINTON POSTMEN. Although slightly out of the area designated for this book, this picture seemed too good to omit. A better Murray Dowding picture, bearing his signature and a date of 1924.

Kingswood and Charfield Cromhall and Wickwar

A BICYCLING BONANZA. A group of cyclists at Kingswood. The men rather outnumbered – 14 to 5, boys included.

THE MEN OF THE ROADS. A county council steam wagon with driver and fireman c.1934. This wagon was kept at the turning to Kingswood, just above Old Farm.

MOBILE HARDWARE. T.J. Hignell & Sons mobile emporium in the 1940s.

KINGSWOOD GARAGE. The legend on the back of this photograph is 1930s, although I would have placed it slightly earlier.

KINGSWOOD SCHOOL. This one is slightly earlier, a postcard view with an actual date.

ABBEY STREET, KINGSWOOD, c. 1905. Are these two pictures a pair? A view from each end of the street, with the Masons Arms on the right in the top picture and on the left in the bottom. Is that the same character watching the photographer? The pictures, both postcard views were taken from different collections.

OUTSIDE THE DOG AND BADGER. This view of c.1910 is one of my favourite pictures. Are these the regulars of the Dog and Badger at Kingswood? What was the occasion? There is hardly a smile on any face with the exception of the second from the right, and by his cider drinking demeanor that smile could well be wind. Perhaps they are all dressed up for an outing and are awaiting the charabanc.

ST. MARY'S CHURCH, KINGSWOOD, C. 1880. Photograph taken before the bell turret was enclosed within a tiled structure.

SITE OF OLD KINGSWOOD ABBEY, C.1905.

NEW MILLS, KINGSWOOD. A beautiful building, and happily still with us today. New Mills was built in 1810 as a cloth mill, there were five water wheels within the mill developing approximately 40 horse power. Note the collars of the tie beams which run between all floors. The photograph here is c.1910.

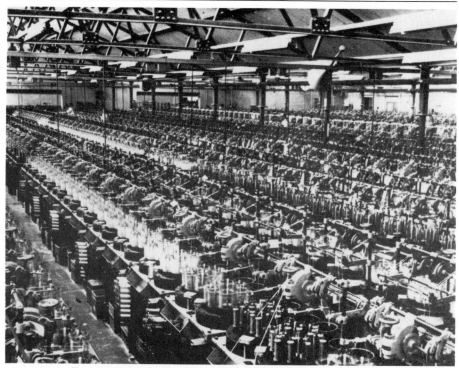

ELASTIC DAYS. Two interior views of New Mills taken some time in the 1950s when Tubbs Lewis made elastic in the mill.

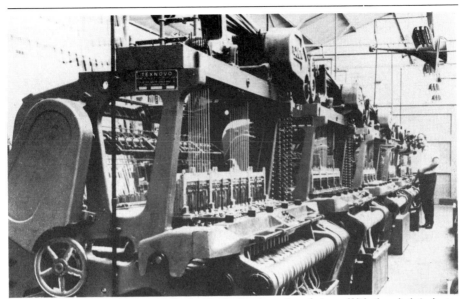

INTERIOR AT NEW MILLS. Two more in the Tubbs Lewis series of views. With the cloth industry failing in the Stroud, Uley, Dursley and Wotton areas, Tubbs Lewis were a very welcome new employer to the area when they set up their elastic manufactory soon after 1870.

THE RAILWAY TAVERN, CHARFIELD. These two views taken a few years apart, probably in the second decade of the century, show the subtle change to take place in this market square. The pub changes its name, horses give way to cars and bowlers give way to flat caps.

CHARFIELD MARKET. This picture is probably contemporary with the bottom view opposite. The doorway to the outbuilding has been blocked up; as against being open and in use as shown as the top view. Apart from this singular fact there are no other identifying indicators; with the exception of the lorry, but even here it could be a new lorry of c.1918, or it could be a ten-year-old lorry of c.1928!

WOTTON ROAD POST OFFICE, CHARFIELD, c.1905.

CHARFIELD STATION, c.1900. Some of these interesting characters are identifiable. Mr Bagwell is the gentleman wearing the straw hat, Mr H. Russell is on the extreme right, Mr Hawley is the station master on the left and one of the others is Mr Hayward.

CHARFIELD STATION. A postcard view of c.1905.

CHARFIELD RAIL DISASTER. 13 October 1928. The frames of burned-out coaches piled up against the bridge.

Considerable mystery surrounds this sad disaster. Five trains were involved. of which only two escaped unscathed. These five were the LMS 10.35pm through freight, Washwood Heath to Bristol; GWR 9.15pm down goods, Oxley Sidings to Bristol; LMS 12.45am down parcels train, Leicester to Bristol, the LMS 10.00pm down passenger and mail, Leeds to Bristol and the 4.45am empty freight, Westerleigh to Gloucester.

The parcels train was overhauling the two goods trains and therefore the LMS goods was shunted into Charfield, and the GWR into Berkeley Road sidings to let the parcels run past. After this, a sequence of misfortunes commenced with the driver of the LMS stopping in Charfield to take on water. Both goods trains came forward, slowed by the delay with the LMS, when the mail train for some unknown reason over-ran the signals and crashed into the GWR, not yet clear of the siding. The empty up train unfortunately arrived on the scene at the time of impact and crashed into the already burning wreckage. The resulting accident claimed 15 lives, two of whom were children – and yet to this day these children remain unclaimed, their identity a mystery.

Most of the deaths were caused by the ensuing fire. The carriages were old rolling stock and all gas-lit. The gas fuelled the blaze. After this accident gas-lit carriages were quite quickly withdrawn throughout the country. The noise of the crash woke up people for miles around. It was heard loudly in Wotton and many rushed to the scene to help, but were unable to get close to the blaze.

CHARFIELD SIGNAL BOX. This picture was taken in L.M.S. days, probably c.1935.

CHARFIELD STATION. L.M.S. locomotive no. 40728 with an 'up' passenger train.

CHARFIELD SCHOOL IN 1928.

STEAMING DOWN THE HIGHWAY! A Wickwar quarries steam wagon c.1925.

BACK TO THE THE RAILWAY TAVERN. A view of the yard c.1922. Obviously madam cannot manage all of her shopping and is admonishing her husband to the amusement of the men standing behind.

RUINS OF OLD MANSION, TORTWORTH. This house was superseded by Tortworth Court in 1852. In this picture it is shown in its last gasp of life.

TORTWORTH COURT. This house was built for the 2nd Earl of Ducie by S.S. Teulon, generally thought of as the most outrageous of the gothic revivalists. The word 'Welcome' carved above the entrance was removed when the house became one of Her Majesty's prisons!

CROMHALL SCHOOL, c.1930.

SODOM MILL, CROMHALL. Two views of the mill c.1910, in one of the early series of pictures from the Cotswold Publishing Company.

Wickwar, High Street from E.

HIGH STREET, WICKWAR. Two similar views, taken about ten years apart. The top picture is c.1915, the bottom one c.1925. The bottom view shows some of the touch-up-artist's licence.

Wickwar, High Street (?).

HIGH STREET, WICKWAR. This earlier view, probably in the first decade of the century shows High Street from the opposite direction to the views on page 110. There is little sign of activity, although from the position of the sun the picture must have been taken at about eleven in the morning.

WICKWAR. This early view c.1900 shows what life was like for pedestrians before the day of the motor car, being able to walk up the unmade-up road in the middle without fear of being run down.

HIGH STREET, WICKWAR. A Postcard view, two lads obviously keeping an eye on the cameraman; c.1910.

Chipping Sodbury, Old Sodbury and Horton

LOVE LANE TURNPIKE. This pikehouse stood at the junction of Love Lane on the Wickwar Road. It was demolished in the early 1970s. This photograph from the Murray Dowding collection was taken c.1910.

HORTON SCHOOL c.1920.

COURT FARM, HORTON c.1920.

HORTON HILL. All of these Horton pictures have been been reproduced from the original glass negatives in the Murray Dowding collection. Unfortunately, although notes, signatures and other descriptions have been scratched on the plates by Dowding, he very rarely put any dates. This view is probably 1925.

HORTON COURT AND CHURCH. Again, the date of this view is uncertain. One of the marks on the plate is 27. This could stand for 1927, or possibly no. 27 in Dowding's filing system.

HORTON VILLAGE, looking up towards the school c.1905. The lad in the straw boater may have been asked to pose by the photographer. Very often cameramen asked for poses to add human interest to otherwise 'dead' images.

TWO VIEWS OF OLD SODBURY. The top picture by Murray Dowding can be dated to c.1908, the picture of the cottage below carries the date 1903. The top cottage was on Old Sodbury Hill, the bottom one in Cotswold Lane.

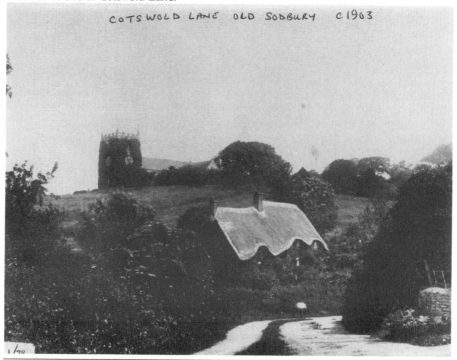

ANCIENT MAN TRAP AT LITTLE SODBURY MANOR. Had it not been from the garb and rough boots, this might almost have been a self-portrait of Dowding. The young man in the picture has the same features, but his face is too sallow.

CHIPPING SODBURY STATION. Or should it be Old Sodbury Station? This was a late arrival to the railway scene, the line from Patchway to Wootton Bassett was an afterthought from the Great Western Railway, and was designed to provide a direct route from South Wales to London with an easier gradient for the coal trains. The building of the railway and the tunnel created considerable prosperity for the town between 1897 and 1903 with more than 600 itinerant workers spending much of their earnings in the area. The line reached full operation on 1 July 1903.

THE GEORGE HOTEL. Men of the 5th Battalion North Lancashire Fusiliers Territorials outside the George in 1914.

CHIPPING SODBURY HORSE PARADE. Outside the George Hotel, Whit Monday 1907.

30/76

MARKET DAY AT CHIPPING SODBURY. This picture was taken from the same position as the horse parade shown on page 121. Probably about eight years later, c.1915. Note the changes in those few years. No major structural changes to buildings have been made, but some of the usages are different. At the end of the street on the left, the Swan has become Powell's Cycle Depot; (see page 125) and other premises have new signs, even if the usage or proprietor has not changed. Note the telegraph poles. The telegraph came into common use in the early 1870s and remained as an important source of speedy messages until the 1940s, after which it has rather petered out – although still available. Its bête noire period was from 1914 to 1918 when for families with young men in the services, the telegraph boy was an unwelcome sight. In the 1907 view on the previous page the telegraph poles are cumbersome concrete post carrying many lines. Presumably by 1915 some modernisation had come about with the increase in telephone users, a service which came to the area just before the turn of the century.

THE RIDINGS QUARRIES BAND. The men in this picture of c.1920 all look very smart. Perhaps some of them are wearing their demob. suits.

THE NATIONAL PROVINCIAL BANK AND POST OFFICE. The National Provincial was one of the 'big five', until the merger with the Westminster Bank some twenty years ago. This picture of c.1909 shows one of those massive telegraph poles immediately outside the post office.

THE SWAN, in its last days as a public house. The sign above the Arnold Perrett & Co. sign reads 'The Swan, by Elizabeth Jane Skiller, licensed retailer of Beer Ale & Cider'. This probably indicates that it was a beer house only, and no spirits or wine would have been available. The building on the right, S.A. & F. Gothard, hairdressers and tobacconists, was slightly remodelled at the front shortly after (see page 122), with a new shop front and porch being added and the whole building tidied up and decorated.

THE SWAN CYCLE WORKS, C.1920. Now no longer a pub, the building looks decidedly shabby.

TWO VIEWS OF THE MARKET, possibly taken on the same day, c.1908. This would appear to be the sheep fair, the pictures are probably by Murray Dowding, but the negatives for these do not appear to be in the archives at Dursley. They were probably sent to the Cotswold Publishing Co. for printing as postcards. Luckily Mr Donald Emes managed to save two good prints before the negatives were destroyed.

THE ROYAL OAK. The sign above the Royal Oak reads 'John H. Dagger, Motors and Cyclists'; groups of thirsty cyclists were obviously good customers c.1908. The picture below is an enlarged detail of the newsagents shop front.

TWO VIEWS OF HORSE STREET. The top view is c.1909 as the Gothard's shop front is still in the old style. The hounds are probably part of the Beaufort Hunt. The bottom view is also of the same date, probably 1909. A few years later large gilt letters were added to the front. On the front of the cart is the name Moses Isaac. Carved above the doorway is the name of the publican, Annie Codrington.

MURRAY DOWDING'S SHOP IN BROAD STREET. These two pictures were taken about sixteen years apart, the top one probably c.1909, the bottom one c.1925. Little appears to have changed in these years, the saddler has gone, but there is no obvious replacement, only a net curtain being at the window. The interesting change is in the subtle alteration of emphasis in the Dowding shop. In the top picture they are advertising themselves as ironmongers. Sixteen years later they have added 'stationer & local views' to the sign, and above that advertise films 'D & P'.

THE PRINCE AND PRINCESS OF WALES, driving through Chipping Sodbury on their way to Yate Station after visiting the Duke of Beaufort at Badminton. Prince George, later George V, did not stop in the town, and one wonders whether the town went rather over the top. The streets were festooned with arches, garlands and greenery, and all the children turned out with their flags to wave and cheer. Presumably they would have used Chipping Sodbury Station if it had been open; at that time it was one year away from completion.

HARRY DANDO'S GARAGE. Harry Dando started his business shortly after the First World War in Hatter's Lane. This picture was taken outside his second premises, also in Hatter's Lane. During the 1930s the business moved to its present site in Rounceval Street. This picture was taken in 1923. The sign advertises open and closed cars for hire. Presumably this included the drivers shown here nonchalantly posing with their right legs up on the running boards. The first two cars are Model 'T' Fords, the older closed vehicle behind is more difficult to identify.

BROOK STREET. These two Francis Frith views of 1903 were published in a small photograph book of Chipping Sodbury. Until the 1700s, Brook Street was the main road into the town from the north.

WHERE BEER IS SOLD BY THE POUND! A Murray Dowding pun. The Boot Inn stood next to a parish pound. This photograph is difficult to date, probably c.1920.

BROOK STREET, c.1910.

THE BAPTIST CHAPEL, in 1903. The chapel was built in c. 1790 and had the new gallery and porch added in 1819.

CHIPPING SODBURY CHURCH. This picture is from a Francis Frith postcard dated 1906.

MILL WALK in 1903. This view is most probably another Frith view. A nicely composed picture, it only lacks human interest. The rather dark reproduction is due to the original being a collotype print from the 1903 Chipping Sodbury book of views.

HORSE STREET in 1903. This picture is also in collotype from the book of local views. The rather fine Georgian buildings on the right seem rather incongruous with the rest of the street. The buildings are not totally Georgian. They were new façades added to older structures.

HATTER'S LANE. This interesting picture of Tudor House was probably taken c.1905. The house is medieval and contains an early fifteenth century stone archway in the hall. It was altered c.1530 and again in the seventeenth century and has features of both periods. By the beginning of this century the building had fallen into a bad state of repair and had become a common lodging house. It was thoroughly restored in 1957.

HATTER'S LANE. This is one of Murray Dowding's early pictures, and one of the few that he dated; 28 July 1910. The building on the left can be seen on page 131 as it later became Harry Dando's garage.

MARKET PLACE in 1903. Another of the collotype printed views of the town. The area on the left hand side of the street had been paved in 1902 after complaints from the Board of Agriculture relating to the hygiene of the market in the town. Markets continued here until 1954.

HIGH STREET. Two views of the street – from opposite sides. The top picture is very faded, but its inclusion in this book can be justified by its age and interest. It must be from before 1871 as the clock tower has not yet been built, and yet gas lamp standards are in place, but the gas works did not commence production until January 1871. Perhaps this detective work shows the picture to be late 1870. The picture below is c.1900.

AN ARMY CONVOY IN BROAD STREET. This picture was taken by Dowding in 1916. Note the sentry guarding the trucks.

BROAD STREET C.1925. The garage on the left was the first in town, opened by Mr J. Penglase in 1919.

IN TIME OF WAR – to use Dowding's commentary on this 1915 portrait of a sentry from the 5th Battalion of the Royal North Lancashire Regiment.

THE CHIPPING SODBURY WORKHOUSE. Dowding uses the term the Guardian's Institution in this picture of c.1920. The workhouse was probably built in 1837 along with others up and down the country following the poor law act of 1834.

BROAD STREET c.1925.

ROUNCEVAL STREET. Two views from the Dowding collection, the top picture looking back into town, the bottom one looking towards Rounceval Street. Both view c.1917.

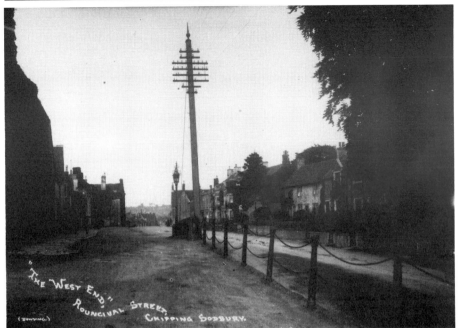

THE WEST END! Where Rounceval Street meets the top of Bowling Hill. The top view by Dowding is one of his few dated pictures, this one was taken 16 June 1917. The picture below is considerably earlier, probably c.1900. The larch tree is shown in both views – considerably larger by 1917!

BOWLING HILL. A view that has changed considerably since this picture was taken c.1910. The house on the left was Chipping Sodbury Vicarage.

Yate and Iron Acton

VIEW AT YATE ROCKS. One of Dowding's better pictures, the country girl with her pail, the labourer plodding his weary way home. Difficult to date, probably c.1920.

NORTH ROAD, YATE c.1935.

YATE STATION, C. 1895. The station was built for the Bristol & Gloucester Railway Company in 1843–4. The contractor was Benjamin Farmer, and the total building contract price was £1,648. On 13 June 1844 the directors and their friends made a trip through the station on route for Stonehouse with *Bristol*, a six-wheeled locomotive, two carriages and a truck. Public traffic commenced on 8 July with six trains a day in each direction.

STATION ROAD, YATE IN 1903.

THE WHITE LION HOTEL. Once in a quiet country lane, the White Lion is now adjacent to a busy shopping centre. This picture was taken in the early 1960s.

POOLE COURT, YATE, renamed from Yate Rectory by the Newman family who took the name from another building called Poole Court, see page 154.

YATE CHURCH AND SCHOOL.

STANSHAWE'S COURT c.1920.

THE RUINS OF YATE COURT. Yate Court Farm was built upon and among the ruins of the court; these date from the end of the thirteenth century. This picture was taken on 14 May 1925. Or, as Murray Dowding has scratched it on the plate 'exposed May 14 1925.'

OXWICK FARM. This curious house was built in 1702 for Mr. Oxwick a citizen and fishmonger of London. Murray Dowding 'exposed' the negative on 17 May 1919.

LATTIMORE FARM c.1920.

POOLE COURT, YATE c.1920. The original Poole Court. See page 151. This building still stands used as offices whereas the second building to carry the name Poole Court has been demolished.

THE GREEN, IRON ACTON. This is number 475 of the Cotswold Publishing Company series. An early series, probably 1909. The name Acton means 'farmstead near the oak tree'. The first recorded date using the prefix 'Iron' was in 1248. The name 'Actune' was recorded in Domesday in 1086. Samuel Rudder in his *New History of Gloucestershire* in 1779 noted that 'great quantities of iron-cinders lying about in several places show that here formerly were iron-works, which probably ceased for want of wood to carry them on.'

THE CROWN AT IRON ACTON. Another Cotswold Publishing Company view, this one numbered 473, also 1909.

IRON ACTON, THE STREET LOOKING WEST. This view is very slightly later. Probably c.1912.

ST. JAMES, IRON ACTON FROM THE EAST. This picture is difficult to date. Because it is a collotype postcard view it is probably no later than 1920s.

ALGARS MANOR c.1912. Originally a Tudor house, the building was substantially altered in the eighteenth century.

OLD COTTAGE AND BRIDGE AT ALGARS MANOR c.1915.

ACTON COURT c.1915. The home of the Poyntz family who were Lords of the Manor from 1344 to 1680. The house was probably rebuilt in the sixteenth century and altered in the seventeenth century although much earlier parts still exist. This was the site of the manor mentioned in Domesday. Originally it was a moated site.

Old Gateway at Acton Court

ACTON COURT.

ACKNOWLEDGEMENTS

My first thanks must go to Mr Donald Emes for allowing the use of his extensive collection, mainly on Wotton-under-Edge, and his help in identifying many pictures. For Chipping Sodbury and Yate I owe much to Mr Jim Elsworth and Mr Percy Couzens who so warmly assisted in my endeavours with this book. For the use of the Murray Dowding collection I am grateful to Mr John Cox and the Gazette Office, where I was allowed to sift freely through the glass negatives, some still in Dowding's original wooden archive boxes.

Finally I thank Mr Simon Herrick and Mr Philip Herrick for kindly advising on identification of the Wotton section.

Errors, omissions and representative imbalance between areas can all be blamed upon me. I have found to my own cost that it is easy to criticize, but not so easy to put a collection such as this together. I know that I must have made many identification errors throughout the book and I would welcome corrections, all of which will be forwarded to Gloucestershire County Record Office to go with a specially hard-bound copy of this book.

Answer to the question on page 51.

> On the extreme right of the building, a leaded window is shown slightly open. These windows were removed during the rebuilding of 1870.

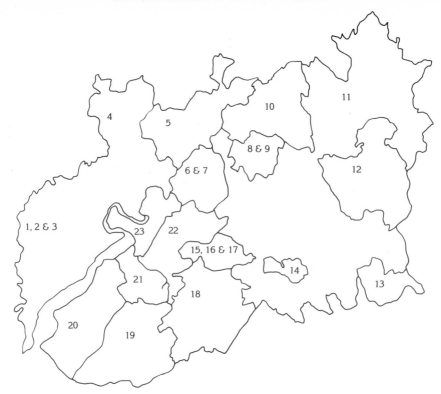